Sew Simple Pinwheels
Karin Hellaby

Quilters Haven
Publications

About the author

Karin Hellaby is the owner of a quilt shop, Quilters Haven, in Suffolk UK housed in a building that dates, in part, to the 1470s. She is a graduate Textiles teacher who enjoys travelling and giving classes all over the world.

As well as writing books, Karin has contributed articles to all the UK quilting magazines. Karin is an adviser for Arena Travel (www.arenatravel.com), a specialist holiday company that has arranged holidays for quilters in Europe and America. In 1998 Karin was the winner of the Michael Kile Scholarship, and International Retailer of the Year.

Karin feels her greatest achievement is to bring up three sons on her own. She started writing books to help support them through University. Ross and Jason are both working in London, and Alexander is completing his final year at Swansea University.

Karin Hellaby

Acknowledgements

This book is dedicated to my three nieces and four nephews. It is a huge pleasure to be part of their lives and to watch as they approach each challenge life throws at them. If only I had my time again with all the knowledge I have gained!

Thanks also to all the makers of the quilts and especially to Kathleen Kerr, my young Canadian member of staff, who has machine quilted most of the quilts and bound many of them, too.

Thanks also to Winbourne, who distribute Moda fabrics in the UK and who sponsored some of the fabric used in the quilts.

First published by
Quilters Haven Publications in 2012

Copyright © Karin Hellaby 2012

Printed by PPG Print, 18-21 Ordnance Court, Ackworth Road, Hilsea, Portsmouth PO3 5RZ

Graphics by Rosemary Muntus
Layout by Allan Scott & Rosemary Muntus

Photography by Roger Barcham,
BMS Imaging Ltd

ISBN 978-09540928-8-7

Quilters Haven Publications
68 High Street, Wickham Market
Suffolk IP13 0QU, UK

Tel: +44 (0)1728 746275
Fax: +44 (0)1728 746314

www.quilters-haven.co.uk

I love playing with block techniques and finding the simplest way to stitch traditional designs. Looking at half square triangles I cut one in two, repositioned the pieces – and suddenly there was a pinwheel!

I drew out my new block onto EQ7. Twisting, flipping and using different colour schemes gave me all sorts of new designs, including some fascinating borders.

Using a slightly different technique I got curved pinwheels, which again could be used in numerous quilt designs. The original pinwheel block really started to spin when spool centres were added. As Suffolk Puffs (also known as yo-yos) are popular, I added these to designs as extra embellishment. I could have gone on creating more and more variations on this block but wanted to work within my *Sew Simple* series.

We have used Charm Squares and Layer Cakes throughout the book as the variety of fabrics in these pre-cut fabric packs can be shown, to great effect, as multi-fabric pinwheels.

Do try this block, maybe add the variations, and send me photos of the lovely quilts you make by starting with a simple pinwheel. Enjoy and create!

Blowing in the Wind *by Teresa Wardlaw (22" × 43")*

Tools and Fabrics

Rotary Cutting Set – Make sure your ruler lines match up with the lines on your cutting board. I like the Omnigrip rulers, as I need a ruler to slide into position and yet not slip when I am cutting. It is useful to have rotary cutting squares for this technique: the 6" square is ideal. Check that all rulers have a 45 degree angle.

Sewing machine – Recommended. Make sure your machine is in good working order. Start a project with a new needle and use a ¼" patchwork foot.

Iron – I normally use a dry iron but found that steam did need to be used to encourage some seams to lie flat – hence the detail given on pressing seams in this book.

Fabric – Use 100% cotton patchwork or dress weight fabrics for best results. Yardage requirements are based on 40-42" wide fabrics. There are many pre-cut bundles of fabric available. Many quilts in this book have been made from Charm Squares (5" fabric squares) and Layer Cakes (10" fabric squares). These can save cutting time and give you a better selection of smaller pieces of fabric.

Marking pencil for use on fabric or **The Angler 2** which eliminates the need to draw a line when making half square triangles.

Threads – Mettler and Masterpiece 100% cotton threads were used for piecing. King Tut threads were the most popular for quilting.

Sharp scissors and pins – I like the long fine quilting pins from Clover and good quality scissors that cut right to the point.

Best Press - A clear liquid starch which helps to give a crisp press when ironing. Ideal for pressing curves.

505 Spray and Fix - Spray basting glue used to layer the quilts ready for machine quilting.

Simple pinwheels

One 7" block requires:

Two 5" squares (pinwheel)
Two 5" background fabric squares

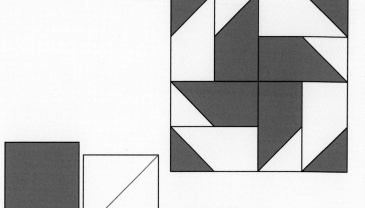

Instructions

1 Mark a diagonal line on the wrong side of the background fabric squares.

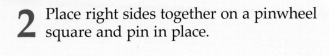

2 Place right sides together on a pinwheel square and pin in place.

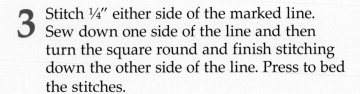

3 Stitch ¼" either side of the marked line. Sew down one side of the line and then turn the square round and finish stitching down the other side of the line. Press to bed the stitches.

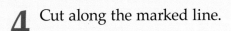

4 Cut along the marked line.

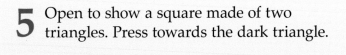

5 Open to show a square made of two triangles. Press towards the dark triangle.

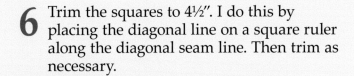

6 Trim the squares to 4½". I do this by placing the diagonal line on a square ruler along the diagonal seam line. Then trim as necessary.

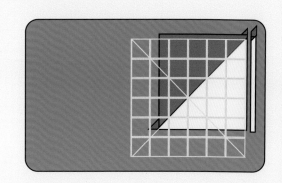

QH tip

Press using the side of the iron and pulling the triangle corner gently.

4

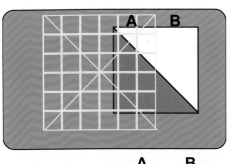

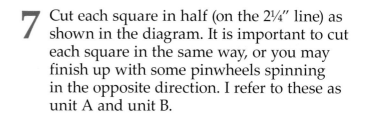

7 Cut each square in half (on the 2¼″ line) as shown in the diagram. It is important to cut each square in the same way, or you may finish up with some pinwheels spinning in the opposite direction. I refer to these as unit A and unit B.

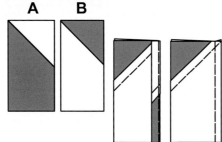

8 Turn unit B as shown and place right side down on unit A. Stitch the two rectangles together. Open to show square, pressing the seam away from unit B.

9 Trim ½″ from the same side of each square to make a 4″ square.

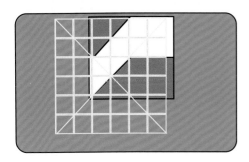

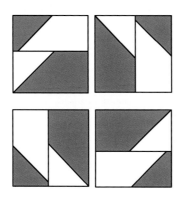

10 Arrange the four squares to create the pinwheel.

11 Sew together in pairs. Press away from outside points.

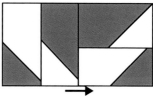

12 Sew pairs together to create a pinwheel block.

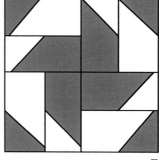

QH tip

Each pinwheel block has several seams meeting in the centre, which can be bulky. To help flatten the centre, make a cut in the last seam allowance so that this seam can be pressed in opposite directions.

Quilt pattern

Dogwood Trail *pieced by Karin Hellaby and quilted by Kathleen Kerr (37½" square)*

Fabric required

1 pack 5" Charm squares (32 are used)

Background fabric: ¾ yard

First border: ¼ yard

Final border and binding: 1 yard

Instructions

1 Lay out the charm squares and group into colours. Each pinwheel is made from two charm squares, in this case two from one colour group.

2 Follow the instructions for Sew Simple Pinwheels (pages 4–5), making sixteen pinwheel blocks.

3 Stitch the blocks together into the quilt top.

4 First border. Cut 1½" strips and stitch to the quilt sides.

5 Final border. Cut 5" strips and stitch to the quilt sides.

6 Layer, quilt and bind following instructions on pages 14–15.

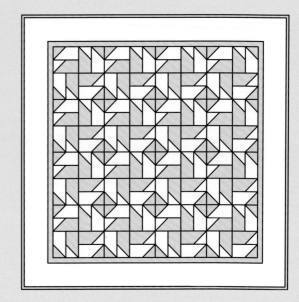

No corners simple pinwheels

One block requires:

Two 5" squares (of pinwheel fabric)
Two 5" background fabric squares
Four 2¼" × 2½" background fabric rectangles

Follow the directions in Sew Simple Pinwheels steps 1-7, pages 4–5. Set aside all unit B. If making multiple blocks for a quilt then these units can be used in a quilt border.

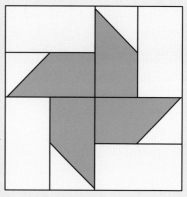

Instructions

1 Stitch a 2¼" × 2½" background fabric rectangle to the long side of unit A.

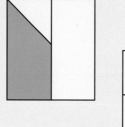

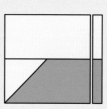

2 Trim ½" from one side as shown to give a 4" square.

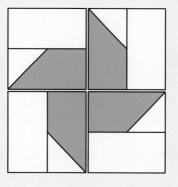

3 Arrange four squares to create the pinwheel effect.

4 Sew together in pairs. Press.

5 Sew pairs together to create a pinwheel block.

How many blocks do you need?

The majority of quilts in this book are between 45-50" square, ideal as crib and wallhanging quilts. For a twin bed size, just double the fabric quantities and make twice the number of blocks. For a king size quilt, make four times the number of blocks.

When planning your quilt you may want to have a line diagram. One is included on the inside front cover, but you can download this and others from www.quiltershavenpublications.com, where you will also find details of the fabric requirements for some of the quilts in this book.

Pinwheel quilts

Canadian Pinwheels *by*
Cheryl Naglis (43" × 43")

Pinwheel Pillow *by*
Pam Lugg, quilted by
Kathleen Kerr
(23" × 23")

Sherbet Kisses *by Georgie*
Smith and quilted by Kathleen
Kerr (41" × 41")

Flowers in the Meadow *by Pam Bailey and quilted by Kathleen Kerr (42″ × 42″)*

Windy City *by Teresa Wardlaw (21½″ × 39″)*

Emperor's Garden *by Karin Hellaby, quilted by Kathleen Kerr, (47″ × 47″)*

Batik table runner *by Karin Hellaby, quilted by Kathleen Kerr (14″ × 54″)*

Curved pinwheels

Layer Cakes or 10" squares are ideal for this technique. Use 5" background squares.

One block requires:

One 10" square, pinwheel fabric
Four 5" background fabric squares
Four 2½" × 5" background fabric rectangles

Instructions

1 Take the pinwheel square and cut into four 5" squares. Fold each square diagonally, right sides out, into a triangle. Press.

2 Lay the folded triangle onto the right side of a background square, matching straight edges. Pin well.

3 To keep these layers aligned, stay stitch the two outside edges with an ⅛" sewing line.

A   B

4 Cut the square in half 2½" from edge. Set aside unit B to use later in a border.

5 Stitch a 2½" × 5" rectangle of the background fabric to each unit A. Press the seam open. Clip the tiny fold of the pinwheel fabric inside the seam.

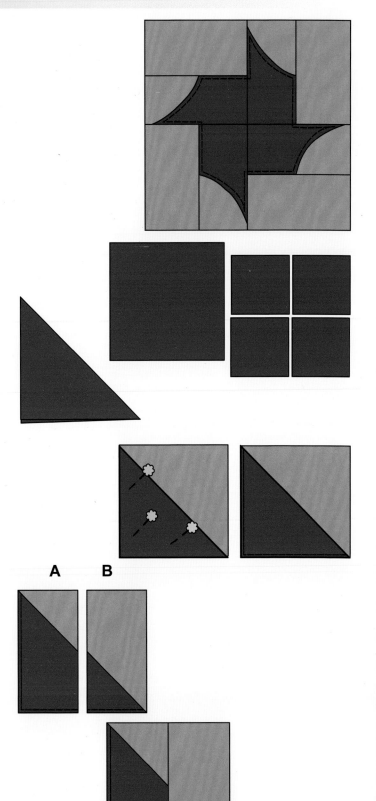

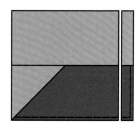

6 Trim the unit to a 4½″ square by removing ½″ from one side of the unit as shown. Repeat to create three more squares.

7 Arrange squares as shown and stitch into a pinwheel block. Press the centre seams open to reduce the bulk.

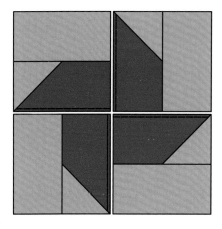

8 Turn and press under the folded edge of the pinwheel blade to form a curve.

9 Top stitch ⅛″ inside the pinwheel, around all the edges.

10 Alternatively the folded edges of each pinwheel may be turned and pressed to the outside forming a curve which can be quilted, beaded or appliquéd into place.

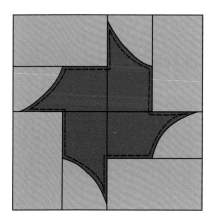

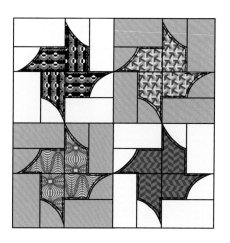

11

Curved pinwheel patterns

Kathleen Wheels

One pack 10" Layer Cake Squares
(25 are used for the pinwheels)

Most Layer Cakes have 40 different
fabrics. From the remaining fabric cut
5" cornerstones and binding strips

Background fabric - 3 yards

Instructions

1 Choose 25 10" squares for the
pinwheels. Cut each into four 5"
squares.

2 Follow the instructions for
Curved Pinwheels, pages 10–11,
making 25 pinwheel blocks.

Kathleen Wheels *by Kathleen
Kerr (48" square)*

3 Stitch the blocks together
into the quilt top.

4 Stitch 20 triangle units into a
border strip. Repeat to make
four borders, as above.

5 Add border strips to two
opposite quilt sides. Press.

6 Stitch a cornerstone to each
end of the two remaining
border strips, and then stitch
these to the quilt top.

7 Layer, quilt and bind
following instructions on
page 14–15.

Red Sails *by Julia Reed*

Spools and Suffolk Puffs

Creating the spool centres

1 Work through stages 1–9 (pages 4–5) to create the 4″ squares.

2 Arrange into units, and for each block cut two 1½″ squares and two 1¼″ squares in contrasting spool fabrics. Lightly spray the backing fabric.

3 Mark a diagonal line on the wrong side of each spool square

4 Place each spool square right sides together on the pinwheel unit, matching raw edges. Pin.

5 Stitch along the marked line. Remove excess fabric leaving a ¼″ seam. Flip the spool fabric over to replace the pinwheel corner.

6 Complete stages 10-12 to make the blocks you need.

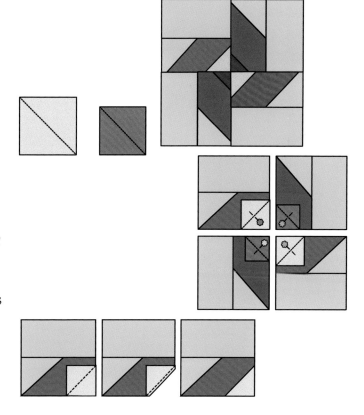

Creating Suffolk Puffs or Yo-yos

1 The traditional method is to cut fabric circles which should be twice the size of the finished puff. Cutting a 5″ diameter circle will give you a 2½″ finished puff.

2 Use a strong quilting thread to gather up the circles.

3 Turn under the circle edge ¼″. Knot the thread and start sewing with the knot under the turned hem. Sew even straight stitches all the way round the circle, turning under the edge as you sew. Overlap the first stitch.

4 Pull up the thread tightly and knot.

5 Flatten the puff so that the 'hole' is in the centre on one side.

I like the yo-yo makers produced by Clover as they are very simple to use and the finished puff is evenly gathered. They come in a variety of sizes, just right for adding extra interest to your quilts.

I stitch a button to cover the 'hole' and then stitch the puff into the quilt.

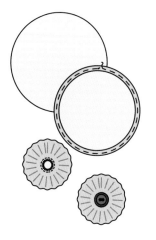

Modern finishing techniques

Layering with 505 spray

A light cotton wadding was used in most of the quilts featured in this book. The quilt layering was done using a 505 Spray and Fix, working one half of the quilt at a time.

1 Lay the backing down wrong side up. Lay wadding on top, then fold back to halfway point.

2 Shake 505 can before using. Hold can 12" from fabric surface. Lightly spray the backing fabric. Using your hand, roll wadding over the sprayed area and firmly press the wadding in place.

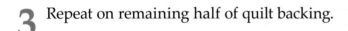

3 Repeat on remaining half of quilt backing.

4 Spray the wadding top, again working one half at a time. Lay the patchwork top onto the wadding right side up, pressing firmly. Repeat with remaining half.

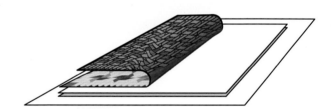

All machined binding

1 Cut binding strips 2¼" wide from your fabric. Stitch into a continuous length using 45° seams. The length of binding should be the circumference of the quilt plus approximately 18".

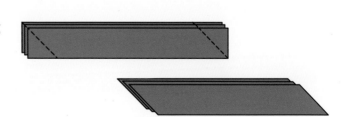

2 Fold and press binding strip in half along length. Joining seams should be pressed open.

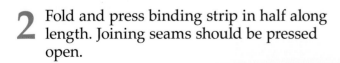

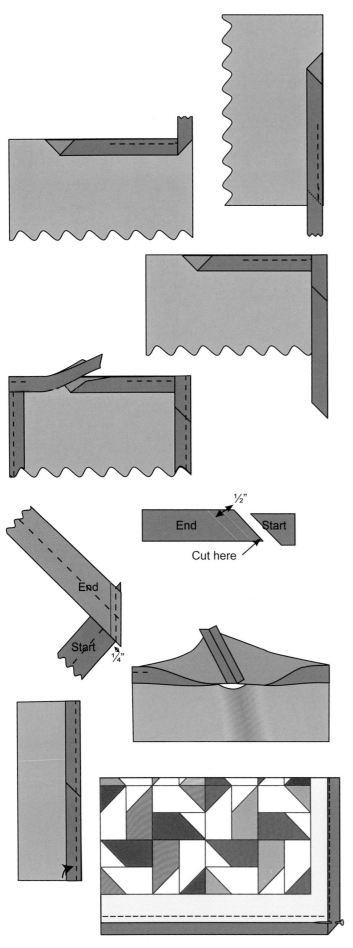

3 Cut the beginning of the binding strip to a 45° degree angle and place on the *back*, halfway down one side of the quilt. Start stitching about 12" from the start of your binding strip, using a ¼" seam.

4 Mitre at each corner. To do this, finish stitching ¼" before each corner, back-stitching to secure the threads. Remove the quilt from the machine and cut the threads.

5 Fold the binding away from you and then towards you, making the fold even with the quilt edge. Pin. Stitch down the side to the next corner and repeat.

6 Finish stitching 12" from where the bindings meet.

7 Lay the folded end binding within the fold of the start binding. Lay flat. Mark the overlap with a line at the same angle as the beginning.

8 Remove from fold and cut any excess binding fabric ½" away from the marked line, using the same angle.

9 Pin the ends of the bindings together, matching raw edges and stitch with a ¼" seam. Press this seam open. Fold back in half and stitch into place.

10 Press binding firmly away from the quilt back.

11 Fold binding to the quilt front and stitch down on the front of the quilt, as close as possible to the binding edge.

12 At each corner use a strong pin to help you fold the corners down neatly as you stitch.

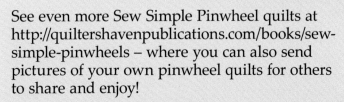

See even more Sew Simple Pinwheel quilts at
http://quiltershavenpublications.com/books/sew-
simple-pinwheels – where you can also send
pictures of your own pinwheel quilts for others
to share and enjoy!